CULTURAL DIVERSITY IN CATHOLIC SCHOOLS:

❖

Challenges and Opportunities for Catholic Educators

Shane P. Martin, SJ, PhD

D1525061

National
Catholic
Educational
Association

© 1996 National Catholic Educational Association, 1077
30th Street, NW, Suite 100, Washington, DC 20007-3852
2nd Printing. 1999

ISBN 1-55833-184-0

TABLE OF CONTENTS

❖

Acknowledgement	vii
Preface	xi
Introduction	1

CHAPTER ONE
Cultural Diversity:
An Important but Problematic Issue — 5

❖ The need for cultural diversity
in education:
Demographic and societal changes — 5

❖ The difficulties inherent
in cultural diversity — 8

CHAPTER TWO
The Success of Catholic Education:
Impressive and Still Able to be Better — 11

The unique success of Catholic
schools in building community   11

Challenges and invitations
for Catholic schools to address   13

    The challenge of diversity
    in the curriculum:
    Multiple perspectives and voices   13

    The challenge of pedagogy:
    Becoming more culturally
    sensitive   15

        Sociocultural theory
        of learning:
        Background   18

        Culturally-sensitive instruction
        and funds of knowledge:
        Teaching to students'
        experience   20

        Culturally-sensitive instruction:
        A constructivist approach
        to learning   23

    The challenge of school culture:
    The importance of a
    welcoming environment   24

        The power of the hidden
        curriculum   24

        Staffing and hiring issues   25

◆ Institutional racism: Addressing areas of cultural mismatch between home and school and the influence of school success or failure   27

CHAPTER THREE
The Catholicity of Our Schools:
Making the Gospel Concrete   31

Conclusion   35

Endnotes

References   38

APPENDIX A
Suggestions for Professional Development
and Faculty In-Service Workshops
Regarding Cultural Diversity   54

◆ Reflection process using this document   55

◆ Focus questions prior to reading the document   55

◆ Reflection questions for the faculty inservice   56

◆ Ongoing reflection activities   57

◆ Review relevant literature   60

◆ Utilize community resources   61

APPENDIX B
Additional Resources for Educators
Interested in Cultural Diversity   63

APPENDIX C
Internet Addresses Concerning
Cultural Diversity   70

ACKNOWLEDGEMENT

❖

There are varieties of gifts, but the same Spirit.

1 Corinthians 12: 4

E Pluribus Unum, the unity that comes from diversity, is a defining value for American civil society. But while most Americans endorse this standard, there are substantial disagreements about exactly what it means.

Plant the flag in the ground and most will rally round, pick it up, and march. Some will follow, while others move out in different directions. Everyone is in favor of diversity, but diversity means different things to different people. So, perhaps, it is not surprising to discover that unity also appears to mean different things to different people.

While unity-diversity debates have a long and checkered history in ecclesial and political arenas, the argument about diversity and schooling has heated up and taken center stage in recent years. It is easy to dismiss extremist positions, but it is also important to acknowledge that many thoughtful and conscientious critics disagree about how educators best serve an increasingly diverse student population.

What role can Catholic educators play in this important national discussion? What can we learn from the work others have done in this area, and what unique contributions can we make in reflecting on our own experiences and our understanding of the mission of our schools? What aspects of Catholic educational practice should be affirmed and identified as models; what elements of our practice need to be evaluated and challenged in order to better serve our mission?

These are large questions, and this is a small book. *Cultural Diversity in Catholic Schools* is an important first step in what will be an ongoing conversation about opportunities and challenges that play an increasingly large role in our agenda for Catholic schools. Father Shane Martin, SJ, brings scholarship and practice together in the context of the Gospel mandate that is the core of our educational mission. He offers sound definitions based on a comprehensive and careful analysis of the literature. His understanding of Catholic schools is based on personal experience as well as research, and is captured in the section entitled *The Success of Catholic Education: Impressive and Still Able to be Better.* In a concluding synthesis, Fr. Martin suggests powerful links between culture, climate and Catholicity. He provides suggestions for faculty discussions and inservice programs and provides an extensive listing of additional resources available from publishers as well as from the Internet. Indeed, this is a small book, but a critically important foundation for the task ahead of us.

This publication was born in conversation between the executive committees of NCEA's departments of elementary schools and secondary schools. An interdepartmental task force provided direction and encouragement for the project. Br. Michael Collins, FSC, president, De La Salle High School, Minneapolis, MN, and Sr. Margaret Ryan, OP, principal, Aquinas High School, Bronx, NY, have represented the secondary schools, while Sr. Katherine Franchett, SCL, superintendent, Great Falls Montana Catholic Schools, and the late Sr. Ernestine L. Gonzalez, STJ, former principal, Sacred Heart School, Uvalde, TX, represented elementary schools.

All of us who are charged to carry this important conversation forward owe a special debt of gratitude to Sr. Ernestine. She brought a great sensitivity to issues of culture, language and socioeconomic status. She was articulate, tireless, and often lonely, but she was always inspiring and hopeful when she talked about the power of Catholic schools to transform lives and to build a just and generous world. In dedicating this book to Sr. Ernestine, we commit ourselves to reflection, discussion and action that will honor her memory and build on her vision.

Michael J. Guerra
Executive Director
NCEA Department of Secondary Schools

Feast of the Assumption, 1996

PREFACE

In the April/May 1996 issue of NCEA's *Momen-tum*, Sister Catherine McNamee, CSJ, former president of NCEA, observed that:

> Catholic education is committed to forming to-day the young people who will be the citizens of the third millennium.
>
> How will we recognize these citizens? They will be imbued with Gospel values; have a clear sense of belonging to the church; conscious of their own human dignity and that of their neighbor; prepared to work toward ending racism, sexism and classism in American society; appreciative of their own cultures; and have a passionate love for all of God's creatures (p. 4).

Undeniably, the extent to which Catholic schools of the next millennium equip young people to work and live in a country populated by an assortment of races and cultures—each mutually respected—will be a prime indicator of those schools' overall quality and of their relevance to contemporary youth and society.

Similar conclusions were reached at the NCEA-sponsored *1991 National Congress on Catholic Schools for the Twenty-first Century.* However, it is one thing to know what our challenges are; it is quite another to know how those specific challenges can be effectively addressed.

Shane Martin knows something about both. As the reader will discover, Father Martin takes seriously the Gospel directive to "teach all nations," and he has successfully translated those words into impressive deeds.

Unless the Church gives witness, through its various agencies, of the love, respect and understanding we should have for all people, it will surely become a stumbling block for many. Those of us who share this opinion have Shane Martin to thank for making that dilemma less likely.

Brother Michael Collins, FSC, EdD
President
De La Salle High School
Minneapolis, MN

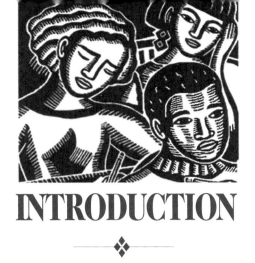

INTRODUCTION

❖

I first began teaching in 1980 as a recent college graduate—young, innocent and full of energy and excitement. Like so many new teachers, I wanted to make a difference in my students' lives. When I graduated from college, I took my first teaching job at a Catholic grammar school in South Central Los Angeles. I taught seventh grade in a school where the children were shaped by all of the influences—positive and negative—in the surrounding community. Our students were very good children; however, many of them had older brothers or cousins who were in jail or in other serious trouble. Many of our students had to struggle to make it; often they had to deal with distressing situations at home, and their parents were trying to do the best they could. My seventh graders tested at the fifth grade reading level as a group, and some of them tested as low as the second grade level. I remember being a first-year teacher, aware of the awesome responsibility of my job, and wondering, "What can I really do to make a difference?".

My second teaching job was after I became a Jesuit, and in a very different setting. I taught for three and a half years at a Jesuit college preparatory high school in the Bay Area of California, in which 98 percent of the graduates went on to college. In this setting, however, were a number of ethnic minority students, many of whom seemed to "fall through the cracks." I was drawn toward working with the ethnic minority students, and with two other faculty members I started a support program for the Latino students at the school. I learned in this experience that it is one thing for a school to have a recruitment and scholarship program for minority students and it is another thing for the school to actually understand and meet their unique educational needs.

For example, I remember a student, Carlos,[1] who was in my Spanish class. Carlos always sat in the back of the classroom with his head down and never looked me in the eye. He was fluent in Spanish, yet he never volunteered an answer and always had a haunted, troubled look on his face. I invited Carlos to join our support program and got to know him very well. Carlos was the oldest of six children; both his parents were born in Mexico. Spanish was spoken at home. Carlos' father never graduated from eighth grade, was an active alcoholic and had been unemployed for seven years. Carlos' mother spoke Spanish exclusively, never attended school and cleaned houses for the family's only income. The family was extremely poor, and although Carlos attended school on a full scholarship plus books, he came to school each day without breakfast and most days had no lunch. When I visited the house one day I looked in the refrigerator when no one was looking and discovered that there was no food. Carlos' extended family lived in the house; he shared a small room with two brothers and two uncles. He had no space in the house to study, no desk or table to do his work. Although he was very intelligent, his grades were not good, and he was in danger of flunking and not graduating.

My years of teaching made me wonder about the *special needs*[2] of ethnic minority, language minority and economically disadvantaged students like Carlos, and how well Catholic schools could respond to these needs.

In this publication I discuss three points concerning ways to better understand and respond to cultural diversity. These three points, which I develop in some detail, are:

(1) The issue of cultural diversity and education is an extremely important and timely topic—particularly for Catholic schools—yet it is a complicated and difficult topic for educators to address.

(2) Catholic schools have done an excellent job in building community, and this has made a notable difference in dealing with cultural diversity. There are still, however, several challenges

and invitations presented to us that we need to address and that we *can* address. We can do so much given our potential.

(3) Catholic schools must address the issue of cultural diversity precisely as Catholic institutions—drawing from our own traditions and legacy. While we must be in dialogue with public schools and be open to learning from educational literature, our ultimate challenge is to integrate current educational practice with the vision and mission of Catholic education.[3]

Shane P. Martin, SJ, PhD

CHAPTER 1

CULTURAL DIVERSITY:
An Important but Problematic Issue

❖

 ## The need for cultural diversity in education: Demographic and societal changes

When I first started teaching at a Jesuit high school in the Bay Area of California in 1983, the student body comprised approximately 90 percent white, European American students. By 1992, when I returned to the school to give a faculty in-service on cultural diversity, the percentage of white students was 63 percent. Such rapid demographic change in the course of a decade underscores the importance of dealing with cultural diversity in education. As the 1990 census made dramatically clear, the United States is a multicultural nation and will become increasingly more so in the future (Martin, 1992a, 1992b, 1993, 1994, 1995/1996; Martin & Artiga, 1994). Presently, one out of four people in the U.S. is a person of color; by the year 2000 it is estimated it will be one out of three (Banks, 1991a). These changes have impacted our Catholic schools: the percentage of ethnic minority students in all Catholic schools has more than doubled during the last 20 years, from 10.8 percent in 1970-1971 to 24 percent in 1995-1996 (Savage, 1996). These numbers are even more dramatic in our large urban centers. In the Los Angeles archdiocese, for example, Hispanic students accounted for 44 percent of Catholic school students in 1991-1992 and all ethnic minority students combined in Catholic schools were 66 percent (Archdiocese of Los Angeles, Department of Catholic Schools, 1992). In many instances we are in situations where the so-called minority is the majority.

Family life and society have also undergone tremendous upheavals in the last 20 years. This is the context in which we are asked to provide education. Consider the following figures compiled in 1993:

- every eight seconds of the school day in the United States a student drops out;
- every 26 seconds of each day a student runs away from home;
- every 47 seconds a child is abused or neglected;

- every 67 seconds an American teenager has a baby;
- every 30 minutes a student is arrested for drunken driving;
- every 30 minutes a youth is killed or injured by guns;
- every 53 minutes a child dies because of poverty;
- every day 100,000 American children are homeless;
- every day six American children commit suicide. (Castruita, 1993)

Additionally:
- in 1955, 60 percent of households in the United States had a working father, a mother at home, and two or more school-age children;
- by 1980 that family unit was only 11 percent of our homes; and
- by 1990 that family unit was only 5 percent of our homes. (Banks, 1991a)

Clearly, the family we once knew will never exist again. Our country has changed dramatically in the past 25 years, and these changes directly impact education. Changes in population and changes in the make up of the family and society have been the impetus for the educational reform movements of the past 15 years. As national scores continue to drop and even more students are marginalized educationally, we must acknowledge that we cannot continue with "business as usual" in our schools. These dramatic changes challenge and invite us to change our way of thinking about education. Cultural diversity is a critical topic for Catholic education.

 ## The difficulties inherent in cultural diversity

Despite all of the good will and good intentions on the part of Catholic educators, the issues involved in cultural diversity are extremely complex and often difficult to grasp fully. For example, when educators speak of cultural diversity it is not always clear *who* is being discussed. The tendency is to lump everyone and everything together in enormous "super groups" which is neither helpful nor precise. When referring to diverse ethnic and cultural groups in the U.S., we speak of African Americans, American Indians, Asians, European Americans and Latinos, without recognizing the many differences within these groups. Japanese, Vietnamese, Filipinos, Koreans, Hmong people, Laotians and Chinese all have very different histories, languages and cultures. Furthermore, Native American Indians number many different nations, each with a different language and history. Additionally, how many teachers have had the experience of having Latino students from different backgrounds in their classrooms—Mexicans, South Americans, Cubans, Puerto Ricans or Central Americans—and found that they are very different as ethnic groups? Similarly, the idea of Anglo homogeneity is also questionable. Are all European Americans alike? The fact is, there is great diversity within diverse groups.

There are also other factors besides ethnicity

that contribute to cultural diversity. As John Ogbu and his associates have illustrated, there are differences in minority experience and status (Ogbu, 1987, 1992a, 1992b, 1993; Ogbu & Matute-Bianchi, 1986). Ogbu indicates that ethnic minority groups have differences in their relationship to the dominant majority, based on differences in group history and levels of assimilation. For example, when I worked with a Latino support program for a Catholic high school, there were notable differences between those ethnic minority students who were born in the U.S. and had assimilated the dominant culture and those ethnic minority students who were born in Latin America and had not yet assimilated.

Language is another very important factor in understanding differences in minority group experience. Some ethnic minority students are English-speaking and others are language minority students, meaning that their primary language outside of school is one other than English. Additional factors such as socioeconomic status make the situation even more complicated. The needs of poor students are very different from advantaged students' needs.

There is so much diversity. However, we tend to group all ethnic minority students together in one category—minority students or students of color—and try to come up with policies and programs that will be helpful to all of them. That just does not work. The educational needs of a newly arrived Central American who does not speak English and the needs of a third-generation Mexican American who was born in the United States and does not speak Spanish are very different, even though they may have the same surname.

In addition to not always knowing *who* we are talking about, we do not always know *what* we are talking about. One problem with multicultural education, for example, is that there are so many different models and definitions that it does not seem that we know what we are doing (Martin, 1993, 1995/1996). This is partly because educational theorists are still developing grounded theory which informs policy and programs in this area. The reality is that educators were not adequately prepared for the demographic changes of the last 25 years, a result of a gap between research and practice. Practitioners have been asked to develop multicultural programs and curricula without having the theoretical foundations in sociology, psychology or anthropology. In many cases, multicultural education has become the next educational fad, and it comes to mean almost anything, or it becomes exclusively identified with superficial methods, such as ethnic foods, ethnic holidays and ethnic heroes (Banks, 1991c).

In summary, it has been very difficult for educators to respond to cultural diversity because there are many ambiguities in terms of who the target group is and exactly what we should do. We, as Catholic school educators, need to be more precise and professional in our efforts in this area.

Chapter 2

THE SUCCESS OF CATHOLIC EDUCATION:
Impressive and Still Able to be Better

❖

 ## The unique success of Catholic schools in building community

This is a very exciting time to be involved in Catholic education. Educators throughout the country are taking a new look at what Catholic schools do and are marveling at the success we have with fewer resources and less money than publicly funded schools. Our success is particularly noteworthy for ethnic minority and "at-risk" students, as studies have documented (Bryk, Lee & Holland, 1993; Coleman & Hoffer,

1987; Coleman, Hoffer & Kilgore, 1982; Greeley, 1982). When I pursued my doctoral studies, I was not sure how it would be for me, as a Catholic priest, to be in a degree program at a private, non-Catholic university whose primary clientele in education were professionals involved in public schools. I received, however, strong support, encouragement and affirmation for Catholic education from my colleagues and professors. The question so many of them asked me was, "How do you do it?". I cannot tell you how many public school principals have asked me that question, in awe of what we have been able to do with so much less.

Catholic schools are doing an outstanding job of building a functional community within the school, and it is this ability to build and sustain community that seems to be a major factor of success. The issue of community is critical to the issue of cultural diversity. Research indicates that a key to success for ethnic minority "at-risk" students is support and motivation (Coleman & Hoffer, 1987; Coleman, Hoffer & Kilgore, 1982; Greeley, 1982), which is central to the Catholic school approach to building community. Many minority students with whom I have worked have told me what they liked best about their Catholic school was that it provided a safe place where they felt valued, affirmed, connected, and at-home. Yet, even though Catholic educators have put forth good efforts in this area, more needs to be done. There are areas of challenge and invitation that still need to be addressed.

Challenges and invitations for Catholic schools to address

There are many challenges to all of us in terms of cultural diversity. This is true for teachers, administrators and educational researchers alike. There are three areas of challenge that are particularly significant for Catholic schools: curriculum, pedagogy and school culture.

 ## The challenge of diversity in the curriculum: Multiple perspectives and voices

Changes in the curriculum are important to consider and yet extremely controversial. From higher educational institutions such as Stanford and Harvard to primary schools and kindergartens, there has been a huge debate in our country about what we teach. One perspective on this issue is shared by those who feel that there is a classic canon of literature that must be learned in order for a person to claim to be educated. Authors from this perspective (Bloom, 1987; D'Souza, 1992; Hassenger, 1992; Hirsch, Kett & Trefil, 1987, 1988; Hughes, 1992; Ravitch, 1990; Schlesinger, 1992; and Steele, 1990, 1992) fear that multicultural education will "water down" the curriculum and divide us as a nation. They fear that the agenda of schools will become the agenda of special interest groups, and this will result in even lower national standards and lower international test scores.

Another perspective is taken by those who propose a diverse curriculum that is more reflective of the cultural pluralism that is the reality

13

in the United States today. This approach, as articulated by authors from this perspective,[4] seeks to present multiple perspectives in the curriculum. These authors argue for a responsible multicultural education that does not aspire to eliminate or replace Western and European perspectives but to augment them with the perspective of voices that are not often heard—Native American Indians, Latinos, Asians, African Americans, and women. For example, what would the notions of manifest destiny and the Westward movement, notions that have traditionally been taught in U.S. schools with uncritical praise and adulation, look like from the perspective of the Native American Indians or the Mexicans who were displaced and whose lives were utterly changed by these forces? What is it like for a young African American student in a Catholic high school to receive a syllabus for literature class and find not one African American author on the list? Or perhaps only one?

Multicultural education remains so controversial because it deals with values and the question of whose voices our students will be allowed to hear. I want to acknowledge that this area is an especially challenging one, and many educators are either willing to give up or to accept anything to pacify oppositional forces. We can do neither. As Catholic educators, it is our responsibility to provide the best education for all students. It is our responsibility to prepare all our students, majority and minority, for a world that is culturally diverse. We need to take a "both/and" approach to curricular innovation. Our curriculum and materials must be chosen because they meet our high standards and because they are educationally appropriate. Additionally, they must reflect the reality of who we are as a people, both as a nation and as Church. Anything less is short-changing our students.

Multicultural education is important because our students need to "see themselves" in the curriculum. Many teachers have told me that parents are increasingly asking about their Catholic school's stance toward diversity at Back-To-School nights. Our parents and students are looking to Catholic schools to make changes in this area. By itself, however, multicultural education is not enough because it mostly involves changes in materials and subject matter. We also need to look at how students learn and how effective our teaching is, especially for ethnic and language minority students.

 The challenge of pedagogy:
Becoming more culturally sensitive

A second area of challenge and invitation is in terms of pedagogy, how we teach. Our own Church documents on education[5] and the documents from Vatican II[6] call us to be open to the "signs of the times" and to the best educational advances and innovations that can complement our Catholic schools. As a 1972 document by the National Conference of Catholic Bishops, *To Teach as Jesus Did*, reminds us:

> The search for new forms of schooling should therefore continue. Some may bear little resemblance to schooling as we have known it; the parish education center; the family education center; the schools without walls, drawing extensively on com-

munity resources; the counseling center, etc...The point is that one must be open to the possibility that the school of the future, including the Catholic school, will in many ways be very different from the school of the past (#124).

A 1982 document from the Congregation for Catholic Education, *Lay Catholics in Schools: Witnesses to Faith,* reminds Catholic educators to update and to learn from educational research, ". . . the Catholic educator has an obvious and constant need for updating: in personal attitudes, in the content of the subjects that are taught, in the pedagogical methods that are used" (#68).

In the past 20 years, educators have often used learning or cognitive styles to focus efforts in responding to cultural diversity. Based primarily on the work of Ramírez and Castañeda (1974), many writers in the field of multicultural education promoted the use of learning styles (Banks, 1988; Bennett, 1995; Gollnick & Chinn, 1994; Lieberman, 1994; Nieto, 1996; Pai, 1990; Scarcella, 1990; Witkin, 1967). Learning style theory holds that people have a cognitive preference for learning, or learning style, by which they best process information and learn. The most popular conception is *field-sensitive* (also called field-dependent) and *field-independent.* Field-sensitive students are described as those who tend to work together for a common goal and are more sensitive to the feelings of others than field-independent students (Banks, 1988, p. 236). Field-independent students prefer to work independently and to compete to gain individual recognition (Banks, 1988, p. 236). Other descriptions of learning styles include *right brain* and *left brain,* and *audio, visual* and *kinesthetic.*

Learning styles have been linked to cultural and ethnic groups (Banks, 1988; Ramírez & Castañeda, 1974). According to this view, European American students are more field-independent while African American, Latino and Native American Indian students are more field-sensitive (Banks, 1988, p. 236). Therefore, teachers should adapt the curriculum and their teaching style to the particular ethnic learning styles of the students within the school community (Banks, 1988, p. 276). The danger with learning styles, however, is stereotyping. As previously discussed, there is much diversity within diverse groups. Not every Latino is field-sensitive nor is every European American field-independent.

Learning style theory fails to address a significant component in educating for cultural diversity—culture is an important factor in education. Culture creates a context for learning, which can vary depending on the activity setting. For this reason, perhaps even more helpful than learning style theory is a theory about learning and teaching that has received increased attention in the last few years and comes from educational anthropology and cultural psychology. In terms of learning this approach is called the *sociocultural theory of learning,*[7] and in terms of teaching it is called *culturally-sensitive instruction* or *culturally-responsive teaching* (Au, 1993).

◆ Sociocultural theory of learning: Background

The sociocultural theory of learning (Au, 1993; Cortés, 1986; Díaz, Moll & Mehan, 1986; García, 1994; Jordan, 1995; Moll, 1990; Rueda, 1987, 1990; Rueda & Moll, 1994; Tharp & Gallimore, 1988; Trueba, 1987; Vygotsky, 1978; Wertsch, 1985a, 1985b) is a theory that addresses the issue of how students learn. The theory brings together several disciplines and draws on the work of the Russian theorist, L. S. Vygotsky, and updates learning style theory by acknowledging the role that cultural context plays in learning. Learning style theory posits universal cognitive styles that are in the individual's head and do not vary from situation to situation. If someone is field-sensitive in one setting, he or she should be field-sensitive in all settings. What this fails to account for, however, is the difference the cultural setting or context can make. Most of us know this to be instinctively true of our own experience—in some settings we are more comfortable than in others, and we act differently when we are comfortable from when we are not.

The sociocultural theory of learning maintains that learning occurs in the interaction between a student, a teacher and the problem to be solved. Both the teacher and student bring something to the process, and the result of their interaction is the construction of knowledge. In this view, knowledge is not a given set of fixed ideas that are passively passed on from teacher to student, but rather knowledge is created by the interaction of the two. An example adapted from Tharp & Gallimore (1988) helps to illustrate this

18

approach. A student comes to her parent and says she has misplaced a textbook. She has looked for it but cannot find it and does not know what to do. The parent does not know where the book is either but begins to ask the student a number of questions, "When did you have it last?", "Where were you yesterday?", "What did you do when you came home?". As the child answers these questions, suddenly she remembers she went into the laundry room after school and that is the last time she remembers having her book. She goes into the laundry room and finds the book. In this example, neither the student nor the parent had the knowledge of where the book was, yet, that knowledge was created in the interaction between the two. They each brought something to the equation. The student brought her experience and memory, and the parent brought remembering skills or meta cognitive techniques.

The sociocultural theory holds that knowledge is socially constructed in the interrelationship between the student, the more competent other (i.e., teacher, parent), and the task at hand. This learning theory says:

- thinking and learning are social processes, not individual processes;
- teaching and learning occur in activity settings where more competent others provide *guided participation* to learners in productive and authentic activities (not task-oriented, decontextualized, abstract and "boring" activities like worksheets or drills);
- learning requires active participation, not passive processing;

- meaningful learning is situated in the context of everyday teaching/learning settings and in everyday problem-solving activities—these vary by cultural context, socioeconomic status and other factors; and
- school failure is a product of the interaction of several factors—the environment, student and teacher—not just the student.

◆ *Culturally-sensitive instruction and funds of knowledge: Teaching to students' experience*

The sociocultural theory is important in discussing cultural diversity because it says that the best way to respond to minority students is with culturally sensitive instruction. In this approach, educators use a student's own experience and cultural background to help create a context for learning. Often described in the literature as *funds of knowledge,* (Floyd-Tenery, González & Moll, 1993; González et al, 1993; Moll & Greenberg, 1990; Moll, Vélez-Ibáñez & González, 1992; Moll, Amanti, Neff & González, 1992; Vélez-Ibáñez, 1988; Vélez-Ibáñez & Greenberg, 1992) this approach maintains that every student walks through the school door with an individual and community-based history and a set of experiences which combined are that particular student's funds of knowledge. It can be described as the totality of experiences and home-based knowledge that each student brings to school from the home culture. Utilizing culturally sensitive instruction and funds of knowledge is especially significant for ethnic minority, language minority and immigrant students because they may bring very different kinds of knowledge and life experience than the dominant majority of students in a school. It is important for teachers to use the existing funds of knowledge that students bring from their families. This helps to build a bridge between the home culture and the school culture and enhances student motivation.

Several examples will help to illustrate the above concept. Educators and researchers in Hawaii were concerned that Native Hawaiians were not scoring well on national standardized tests. A group of educators, anthropologists and psychologists spent several years observing the native culture to understand how learning occurred naturally in the home community. They used their findings to create a model school, the Kamehameha Early Education Project (KEEP), which featured culturally sensitive instruction. Incorporating such native cultural practices such as the "talk story," the teachers focused on building literacy for the students, utilizing their funds of knowledge and employing teaching strategies and techniques that were compatible with the way students learned in their homes, such as cooperative learning. The results were dramatic increases in literacy as measured on national standardized tests (Au, 1980, 1992; Au & Kawakami, 1985, 1986, 1991; Tharp & Gallimore, 1988; Jordan, Tharp, Baird-Vogt, 1992; Vogt, Jordan & Tharp, 1987).

Another example is from the KEEP-Rough Rock Project which attempted to transfer the success of KEEP to another setting. The teachers at Rough Rock were working with Navaho

21

students and were frustrated because they could not get the students to understand difficult and abstract mathematical concepts. These Navaho were sheep herders and farmers. When the teachers changed the context and presented the mathematical concepts in terms of real-life problems involving numbers and percentages with sheep and crops, however, not only did the students learn these concepts but they were able to master them. This knowledge transferred to other areas of abstract mathematical thinking, and these students improved overall (Jordan, Tharp & Vogt, 1985).

Another example comes from a colleague who was teaching first year writing at a secondary school in East Los Angeles. She had a particularly difficult time in motivating one of her students to write. As she learned more about this student and what interested him, she designed assignments to fit his experience. Soon this student was writing incredible essays about cars, about low riders and hydraulics, and the teacher had an entrée to work with him in the areas of grammar and style. A Latino student at a Catholic school in San Jose was completely bored with poetry and literature, until the teacher found several poems and short stories that were about his Chicano experience. Suddenly, this student who had only gotten C's was earning A's in English.

A final example is those certain students who say they cannot understand mathematic and scientific concepts, yet they can recite from memory any number of pitchers' ERAs, players' batting averages, percentage of free-throws made by a team, or the complicated and intricate rules of football. Often these same students cannot give an oral report in the classroom, yet they can passionately and articulately discuss at length who is going to the NCAA's Final Four Basketball Tournament and why, offering well-thought-out positions based on facts, figures and logic. In all of these cases, students have funds of knowledge based on their home-cultures or other life experiences.

◆ Culturally-sensitive instruction: A constructivist approach to learning

The key to culturally-sensitive instruction is building a bridge from a student's experience, home culture and funds of knowledge to the school culture. In using this approach toward teaching, educators affirm and recognize a student's cultural identity and background. This does not mean that teachers never use abstract, decontextualized instruction; all students must learn to master these areas as well, but that is not the starting point. We need to get students motivated and excited about learning. Starting with their own funds of knowledge and connecting instruction to meaningful, context-sensitive activities in the everyday experiences of our students is a good way to motivate (Rueda & Moll, 1994).

For example, in history students can research their family background and make a family tree, write a family history or complete a historical family interview project. In English students can write from their experience about topics that come from their culture and their world. In math teachers can create projects that examine the number of immigrants from a particular country in a longitudinal study and chart the percentage of those immigrants who live below the poverty line in the U.S. In science we can use a problem-solving approach to motivate students and to help them think about scientific notions, an approach that Stigler & Stevenson (1991) found to be successfully employed by Asian teachers. As educators we must be creative and imaginative as well as culturally sensitive. Students can be co-creators of these types of projects with us.

 ## The challenge of school culture: The importance of a welcoming environment

 ### The power of the hidden curriculum

The third area in which we are challenged and invited to respond to cultural diversity concerns the school culture. In every school there is both an explicit curriculum and what Philip Jackson (1968) referred to as the *hidden curriculum*. The hidden curriculum consists of the values, beliefs and messages we give our students in the informal, non-instructional areas that permeate the entire school culture. This is an excellent area for all those involved with education to consider—what is the hidden curriculum in our classrooms? In our schools? What is the school environment like for ethnic minority students? What kinds of things do we put on the walls of our schools and classrooms? Do ethnic and language minority students feel valued and connected to the school? These questions reflect the power and importance of the hidden curriculum.

All students need to be able to "see themselves" in some way in the school culture. If ethnic minority students are unable to see themselves in the school's curriculum or activities, composition of the faculty or staff, or the school culture, then school can become a distancing place. Every student has the right to feel connected to the school, to feel some sense of ownership, that this is "my" school. At times school officials are not aware that ethnic and cultural minority students are having a difficult time in terms of relating to the hidden curriculum of the school. It is important for educators to regularly evaluate the school's progress in this area, especially to elicit feedback from students.

◆ *Staffing and hiring issues*

One of the concerns in the area of school culture pertains to staffing and hiring. Are there adequate ethnic minority role-models for students? I once worked in an all-male Catholic high school which was nine percent Latino students, and the only Latino males on the faculty or staff of approximately 100 were the six Mexican custodians. Such an arrangement can give a very subtle and unintended message to the Latino students at the school: the only place for you is working as a custodian. Another example is a Catholic high school that is nineteen percent Asian students. A young Vietnamese Jesuit was assigned to work at this school. A Vietnamese student told another faculty member that he was stunned the first time he saw this Jesuit dressed in clerics because, until that moment, he never thought that being a priest or a teacher was an option for him. He had never before seen an Asian priest or teacher.

It is important for all students, majority and minority, to have the experience of working with ethnically diverse faculty, staff and administrators. A good situation is one where the ethnic composition of the faculty and staff roughly reflects the population in the community. Some administrators in Catholic schools have expressed frustration in their attempts to diversify the faculty and staff, claiming, "They just are not out there.". However, upon further reflection, what most of the administrators really mean to say is that ethnic minority candidates do not readily apply to their schools using the regular procedures and application process.

Diversity of faculty and staff is an important educational value, and administrators need to make this an important consideration in hiring. Some schools have successfully targeted ethnic minority alumni and engaged them in supportive relationships while encouraging them through college and teacher education programs. Another possibility is creating links with schools of education and teacher training programs to identify students early in their careers. Finally, schools with the most success in this area have developed bonds with ethnic minority communities. Rather than waiting for candidates to apply, some administrators go into home communities to recruit and encourage people of color to consider teaching at a Catholic school. A proactive stance seems to be the most successful.

Institutional racism: Addressing areas of cultural mismatch between home and school and the influence of school success or failure

Sometimes institutions, without being aware, take on aspects of institutional racism. This happens when we ask our ethnic and language minority students to stop being who they are in order to become something else that we espouse to be better. This happens when we tell non-English speaking parents that they should not speak their native language at home because it might confuse the children. Research in this area clearly and emphatically shows that forcing students to completely abandon their primary language impedes the students' language acquisition and cognitive abilities (Arias & Casanova, 1993; Cummins; 1986, 1989; Crawford, 1989, 1991; Krashen, 1985; Krashen & Biber, 1988). One widely read book, *Hunger of Memory* by Richard Rodriguez (1982) discusses issues related to second language. A chilling moment in the book occurs when two religious sisters visit the family's home and tell the parents they must never speak Spanish to their children because it impairs their English development. The mother announces that from that moment on only English would be spoken in the home. Sadly, as Rodriguez recounts, that moment ends family discussions at the dinner table, meaningful conversation with the parents and all conversation with the grandparents. Today, unfortunately, there are still teachers who give a similar message about language to parents and students.

27

Institutional racism also happens when educators do not address the cultural discontinuities between the home culture and the school culture but assume that ethnic and linguistic minority students come to school from an impoverished and deficient background and need "to be fixed." This attitude sets up a dynamic that only increases the chances of school failure for children from culturally diverse backgrounds. We force students to choose between their home culture and the school culture (McDermott, 1987). From this perspective, school failure often occurs because minority students perceive that there are no real alternatives for them. They feel that, because of inherent racism and prejudice in our schools and in society, doing well in school will not be a realistic way to change their status as a minority (Ogbu, 1992b). As McDermott (1987) noted:

> School failure and delinquency often represent highly motivated and intelligent attempts to develop the abilities, statuses, and identities that will best equip the child to maximize his (or her) utilities in the politics of everyday life. If the teacher is going to send degrading messages regardless of how the *game* is played, the child's best strategy is to stop playing the game (p. 204).

The issue is one of an assimilationist perspective versus a cultural pluralistic perspective. Many fear that if we as a people in the U.S. do not have common values, a common language, and a common sense of peoplehood, then we will not hold together as a nation. At issue is the question of who decides what the common values are and what the common sense of

28

peoplehood will be. A strict assimilationist perspective feels that home cultures and languages must cease and that everyone must become "American." The difficulty with this approach, however, is that in a democracy such as the United States, there are many different legitimate expressions of what it is to be an American. A culturally pluralistic perspective maintains that the United States has always been a nation of diverse cultures, and that is precisely what being "American" means. It is the question of being able to hold diversity and unity together, of being able to take a "both/and" approach to cultural diversity (Cortés, 1994).

A strict assimilationist model, which says to minority students, "You must lose your ethnic culture and language and become anglicized" is much too heavy-handed an approach. So how do educators in Catholic schools hold these seemingly contradictory values together? I think the answer to this is in our own tradition and legacy as the Catholic Church. Ultimately the way we will deal with this issue has to be faithful to our own values and mission as Catholic schools.

CHAPTER 3

THE CATHOLICITY OF OUR SCHOOLS:
Making the Gospel Concrete

❖

Many people define cultural diversity as "anything goes;" that there are no commonly held and shared values. This is not necessarily true. We do need to set a standard because our schools have a specific moral purpose. The standard, however, should be in terms of Catholic values, not assimilation.

Catholic school values are Gospel values. If we look to the life and ministry of Jesus, we see that he embodied these values. Jesus was available to all, yet he took a special option for those who were marginalized in the society of his day—the tax collector, the prostitute, the leper, the woman caught in adultery. There are many examples of how Jesus dealt with those who were ethnically or culturally different from the dominant culture—the good Samaritan, the Centurion, the Samaritan woman at the well. He always treated them with dignity and respect. The hero of the good Samaritan story turns out to be a member of the ethnic group most despised by the dominant majority.

Jesus called people as they were with their own experiences and funds of knowledge. An example is the way he related to Peter, using Peter's own history and background as the very method in which he taught him. Peter was a fisherman; Jesus lured him in with the miracle of the great catch and later told him he would be catching men and women in his nets. Jesus accepted the woman who anointed his feet and dried them with her hair. He treated Matthew the tax collector, the woman at the well, and the woman caught in adultery with empathy and compassion by relating to their experiences. There was room under his umbrella of ministry for diversity.

This is not to say that Jesus did not challenge his followers. He challenged them every step of the way: to think more reflectively and live lives that modeled justice and compassion. He never did so by coercion. His method was attraction and invitation. We are called to do the same thing in our Catholic schools. Diversity does not mean we let go of our standard, which is to form other-centered men and women who can make a difference in this world, but that we use what our students bring—their home culture and their funds of knowledge—and we gently but deliberately invite them to live their lives according to the Gospel. For us to do anything less would be to sell out on our mission of being Catholic schools. If we want a model of culturally-sensitive instruction, all we need to do is to look to the Gospels.

CONCLUSION

❖

I would like to return to the story of Carlos mentioned earlier. I had said that Carlos was in danger of flunking. Several teachers intervened and provided Carlos with the extra support and encouragement he needed. We set up an individual tutoring program for him and created his own study hall. We facilitated meetings with all of his teachers and got him back on track in his classes. We sat down with him and his parents to discuss college plans and assisted them in filling out the proper forms. Carlos received a full scholarship and attended college. He graduated and is now pursuing a master's degree. He is thinking of going to law school, and not too long ago he asked me if, after he was a lawyer, he could endow a scholarship at his Catholic high school for a low-income ethnic minority student like himself.

ENDNOTES

❖

1. All names used in this chapter are pseudonyms.

2. The term *special needs* refers to the unique needs that ethnic minority, language minority, poor or physically or mentally challenged students have that could affect the educational process if not recognized and met. At times these needs are kept from the sight or knowledge of others, due to several factors such as institutional racism, cultural mismatch, or cultural insensitivity.

3. The author wishes to thank Dr. Robert Rueda of the University of Southern California for his helpful suggestions regarding this chapter, Elizabeth Wholihan for editorial assistance, and Ernesto Colin for research assistance.

4. To learn more about offering diverse curriculum that reflects the cultural pluralism in the U.S. today, please see American Association of Colleges for Teacher Education [AACTE], 1973; Baker, 1994; Banks, 1983a, 1983b, 1988, 1991b, 1991c, 1993a, 1993b, 1993c; Banks & Banks, 1993; Baptiste, 1977; Baptiste, Baptiste & Gollnick, 1980; Bennett, 1995; Campbell,

1996; Garcia, 1993; Gay, 1977, 1979, 1983a, 1983b, 1983c, 1988; Gollnick & Chinn, 1994; Gollnick, Klassen & Yff, 1976; Grant & Gomez, 1996; Grant & Sleeter, 1985; Grant, Sleeter & Anderson, 1986; McCarthy, 1993; Nieto, 1996; Payne, 1983; Sleeter, 1989, 1991, 1993; Sleeter & Grant, 1987, 1988; Sleeter & McLaren, 1995, Scarcella, 1990; Suzuki, 1984.

5. See, for example, The Catholic School (Congregation for Catholic Education, 1977); Lay Catholics in Schools: Witnesses to Faith (Congregation for Catholic Education, 1982); To Teach as Jesus Did (National Conference of Catholic Bishops, 1972).

6. See, for example, The Documents of Vatican II (Abbott, 1966), especially "The Church in the Modern World."

7. While several educational theories are "sociocultural" in the broad sense that they deal with aspects of society and culture, this paper refers to the neo-Vygotskian school of sociocultural theorists.

REFERENCES

❖

Abbott, W. M. (Ed). (1966). The Documents of Vatican II (J. Gallagher, Trans.). New York: Guild Press.

American Association of Colleges for Teacher Education/Commission on Multicultural Education. (1973). "No One Model American." The Journal of Teacher Education, 24, 264-265.

Archdiocese of Los Angeles Department of Catholic Schools. (1992). Census summary: 1992-1993. Los Angeles: Author.

Arias, M. B., & Casanova, U. (Eds.). (1993). Bilingual Education: Politics, Practice, and Research. Ninety-second yearbook of the National Society for the Study of Education. Chicago: University of Chicago Press.

Au, K. H. (1980). "Participant Structure in a Reading Lesson with Hawaiian Children: Analysis of a Culturally Appropriate Instructional Event." Anthropology and Education Quarterly, 11, 91-115.

Au, K. H. (1992). "Constructing the Theme of a Story." Language Arts, 69, 106-111.

Au, K. H. (1993). Literacy Instruction in Multicultural Settings. Fort Worth, TX: Harcourt Brace College Publishers.

Au, K. H., & Kawakami, A. J. (1985). "Research Currents: Talk Story and Learning to Read." Language Arts, 62, 406-111.

Au, K. H., & Kawakami, A. J. (1986). "Influence of the Social Organization of Instruction on Children's Text Comprehension Ability: A Vygotskian Perspective." In T. E. Raphael (Ed.), The Contexts of School Based Literacy (pp. 63-77). New York: Random House.

Au, K. H., & Kawakami, A. J. (1991). "Culture and Ownership: Schooling of Minority Students." Childhood Education, 67, 280-284.

Baker, G. C. (1994). Planning and Organizing for Multicultural Education (2nd ed.). Menlo Park, CA: Addison-Wesley.

Banks, J. A. (1983a, April). "Multiethnic Education and the Quest for Equality." Phi Delta Kappan, 64, 582-585.

Banks, J. A. (1983b, April). "Multiethnic Education at the Crossroads." Phi Delta Kappan, 64, 559.

Banks, J. A. (1988). Multiethnic Education: Theory and Practice (2nd ed.). Boston: Allyn and Bacon.

Banks, J. A. (1991a, October-November).

Background Perspective and Need for Multicultural Education. Paper presented at the National Conference on Multicultural Education, New Orleans, LA.

Banks, J. A. (1991b). "Multicultural Literacy and Curriculum Reform." Educational Horizons, 69, 135-140.

Banks, J. A. (1991c). Teaching Strategies for Ethnic Studies (5th ed.). Boston: Allyn and Bacon.

Banks, J. A. (1993a). "The Canon Debate, Knowledge Construction, and Multicultural Education." Educational Researcher, 22(5), 4-14.

Banks, J. A. (1993b). "Multicultural Education: Development, Dimensions, and Challenges." Phi Delta Kappan, 75, 22-28 James A. Banks (Ed.).

Banks, J. A. (1993c). "Multicultural Education: Historical Development, Dimensions, and Practice." In L. Darling-Hammond (Ed.), Review of Research in Education (Vol. 19, pp. 3-50). Washington, DC: American Educational Research Association.

Banks, J. A., & Banks, C. A. (Eds.). (1993). Multicultural Education: Issues and Perspectives (2nd ed.). Boston: Allyn and Bacon.

Baptiste, H. P. (1977). "Multicultural Education Evolvement at the University of Houston: A Case Study." In F. H. Klassen & D. M. Gollnick (Eds.), Pluralism and the American Teacher: Issues and Case Studies. Washington, DC: American Association of Colleges for Teacher Education.

Baptiste, H. P., Baptiste, M. L., & Gollnick, D. M. (Eds). (1980). Multicultural Teacher Education: Preparing Educators to Provide Educational Equity. Washington, DC: American Association of Colleges for Teacher Education.

Bennett, C. I. (1995). Comprehensive Multicultural Education: Theory and Practice (3rd ed.). Boston: Allyn and Bacon.

Bloom, A. (1987). The Closing of the American Mind. New York: Simon & Schuster.

Bryk, A. S., Lee, V. E., & Holland, P. B. (1993). Catholic Schools and the Common Good. Cambridge, MA: Harvard University Press.

Campbell, D. E. (1996). Choosing Democracy: A Practical Guide to Multicultural Education. Englewood Cliffs, NJ: Merrill.

Castruita, R. (1993). Multicultural Education: Here They Come—Ready or Not. Paper presented at the 39th Annual Society of Delta Epsilon Lecture, University of Southern California, Los Angeles.

Coleman, J. S., & Hoffer, T. (1987). Public and Private Schools: The Impact of Community. New York: Basic Books.

Coleman, J. S., Hoffer, T., & Kligore, S. (1982).

High School Achievement: Public, Catholic, and Private Schools Compared. New York: Basic Books.

Congregation for Catholic Education. (1977). The Catholic School. Boston: St. Paul Editions.

Congregation for Catholic Education. (1982). Lay Catholics in Schools: Witnesses to Faith. Boston: St. Paul Editions.

Cortés, C. E. (1986). "The Education of Language Minority Students: A Contextual Interaction Model." In Beyond Language: Social and Cultural Factors in Schooling Language Minority Students (pp. 3-34). Los Angeles: Evaluation, Dissemination and Assessment Center, California State University, Los Angeles.

Cortés, C. E. (1994). "Limits to *pluribus*, Limits to *Unum*: Unity, Diversity and the Great American Balancing Act." Phi Kappa Phi Journal, 74(1), 6-8.

Crawford, J. (1989, May). "Appreciating diversity." Hispanic, pp. 52-53.

Crawford, J. (1991). Bilingual Education: History, Politics, Theory and Practice (2nd ed.). Los Angeles: Bilingual Educational Services.

Cummins, J. (1986). "Empowering Minority Students: A Framework for Intervention. Harvard Educational Review, 56, 18-36.

Cummins, J. (1989). Empowering Minority

Students. Sacramento, CA: California Association for Bilingual Education.

Díaz, S., Moll, L. C., & Mehan, H. (1986). "Sociocultural Resources in Instruction: A Context-specific Approach. In Beyond Language: Social and Cultural Factors in Schooling Language Minority Students (pp. 187-230). Los Angeles: Evaluation, Dissemination and Assessment Center, California State University, Los Angeles.

D'Souza, D. (1992). Illiberal Education: The Politics of Race and Sex on Campus. New York: Random House.

Floyd-Tenery, M., González, N., & Moll, L. C. (1993, November). "Funds of Knowledge for Teaching (FTK) Project: A Replication and Update" [On-line]. The Electronic Bulletin Board. (Available Gopher: National Center for Research on Cultural Diversity and Second Language Learning, 128.111.206.1, GSE Information and Resources).

García, E. E. (1993). "Language, Culture, and Education." In L. Darling-Hammond (Ed.), Review of Research in Education (Vol. 19, pp. 51-98). Washington, DC: American Educational Research Association.

Garcia, J. (1993). "The Changing Image of Ethnic Groups in Textbooks." Phi Delta Kappan, 75, 29-35.

Gay, G. (1977). "Curriculum Design for Multicultural Education." In C. Grant (Ed.),

<u>Multicultural Education: Commitments, Issues and Applications.</u> Washington, DC: Association for Supervision and Curriculum Development.

Gay, G. (1979). "Changing Conceptions of Multicultural Education." In H. Baptiste & M. Baptiste (Eds.), <u>Developing Multicultural Process in Classroom Instructions: Competencies for Teachers</u> (pp. 18-30). Washington, DC: University Press of America (Reprinted from Educational Perspectives, December, 1977, published by University of Hawaii, Honolulu, HI).

Gay, G. (1983a). "Multiethnic Education: Historical Developments and Future Prospects." <u>Phi Delta Kappan,</u> 64, 560-563.

Gay, G. (1983b, February). "Retrospects and Prospects of Multicultural Education." <u>Momentum,</u> pp. 5-8.

Gay, G. (1983c). "Why Multicultural Education in Teacher Preparation Programs." <u>Contemporary Education,</u> 54(2), 79-85.

Gay, G. (1988). "Designing Relevant Curricula for Diverse Learners." <u>Education and Urban Society,</u> 20, 327-340.

Gollnick, D. M., & Chinn, P. C. (1994). <u>Multicultural Education in a Pluralistic Society</u> (4th ed.). New York: Merrill.

Gollnick, D. M., Klassen, F. H., & Yff, J. (1976). <u>Multicultural Education and Ethnic Studies in the United States: An Analysis and Annotated</u>

Bibliography of Selected ERIC Documents. Washington, DC: American Association of Colleges for Teacher Education; ERIC Clearinghouse on Teacher Education.

González, N., Moll, L. C., Floyd-Tenery, M., Rivera, A., Rendón, P., Gonzales, R., & Amanti, C. (1993). Teacher Research on Funds of Knowledge: Learning from Households. (Educational Practice Report: 6). Santa Cruz, CA: National Center for Research on Cultural Diversity and Second Language Learning.

Grant, C. A., & Gomez, M. L. (Eds.). (1996). Making School Multicultural: Campus and Classroom. Englewood Cliffs, NJ: Merrill.

Grant, C. A., & Sleeter, C. E. (1985). "The Literature on Multicultural Education: Review and Analysis." Educational Review, 37(2), 97-118.

Grant, C. A., Sleeter, C. E., & Anderson, J. E. (1986). "The Literature on Multicultural Education: Review and Analysis." Educational Studies, 12(1), 47-71.

Greeley, A. M. (1982). Catholic High Schools and Minority Students. New Brunswick: Transaction Books.

Hall, G., E., & Hord, S. M. (1987). Change in Schools: Facilitating the Process. SUNY Series in Educational Leadership. New York: State University of New York Press.

Hassenger, R. (1992). "True Multiculturalism:

Setting no Boundaries." <u>Commonweal,</u> 69(7), 10-11.

Hirsch, E. D., Kett, J., & Trefil, J. (1987). <u>Cultural Literacy: What Every American Needs to Know.</u> Boston: Houghton Mifflin.

Hirsch, E. D., Kett, J., & Trefil, J. (1988). <u>The Dictionary of Cultural Literacy.</u> Boston: Houghton Mifflin.

Huberman, M., & Miles, M. (1984). <u>Innovation up Close: How School Improvement Works.</u> New York: Plenum.

Hughes, R. (1992, February 3). "The Fraying of America." <u>Time,</u> pp. 44-49.

Jackson, P. W. (1968). <u>Life in Classrooms.</u> New York: Holt, Rinehart and Winston.

Jordan, C., Tharp, R. G., & Vogt, L. (1985). <u>Compatibility of Classroom and Culture: General Principles, with Navajo and Hawaiian Instances.</u> Unpublished manuscript.

Jordan, C. (1995). "Creating cultures of schooling: Historical and conceptual background of the KEEP/Rough Rock collaboration." <u>Bilingual Research Journal,</u> 19(1), 83-100.

Jordan, C., Tharp, R. G., & Baird-Vogt, L. (1992). "Just Open the Door: Cultural Compatibility and Classroom Rapport." In M. Saravia-Shore & S. F. Arvizu (Eds.), <u>Cross-cultural Literacy: Ethnographies of Communication in</u>

Multiethnic Classrooms (pp. 3-18). New York: Garland Press.

Krashen, S., & Biber, D. (1988). On Course: Bilingual Education's Success in California. Sacramento, CA: California Association for Bilingual Education.

Krashen, S. D. (1985). The Input Hypothesis: Issues and Implications. Torrance, CA: Laredo.

Lieberman, D. A. (1994). "Ethnocognitivism, Problem Solving, and Hemispericity." In L. A. Samovar & R. E. Porter (Eds.), Intercultural Communication: A Reader (7th ed., pp. 178-193). Belmont, CA: Wadsworth.

Martin, S. P. (1992a). Multicultural Education and Catholic Schools: A Faculty In-service Program. Unpublished master's thesis, Jesuit School of Theology at Berkeley, Berkeley, CA.

Martin, S. P. (1992b, April). Multicultural Education and Catholic Schools: Issues and Challenges. Paper presented at the Dean's Lecture Series, Jesuit School of Theology, Berkeley, CA.

Martin, S. P. (1993). "The Problem of Multicultural Education: Background, Definitions and Future Agenda." Multicultural Education Journal, 11(1), 9-20.

Martin, S. P. (1994, April). Cultural Diversity in Catholic Secondary Schools: Issues, Challenges and Invitations. Paper presented at the National Catholic Education Association Annual

Convention, Anaheim, CA.

Martin, S. P. (1996). The Relationship of Cultural Diversity to Jesuit Secondary Education in the United States: A Theoretical and Case Study Analysis (Doctoral Dissertation, University of Southern California, Los Angeles, 1995). Dissertation Abstracts International, 57(01), 79-A, DA9614047.

Martin, S. P., & Artiga, E. S. (1994). "A Faculty In-service Affirms Cultural Diversity." Momentum, 25(2), 28-31.

McCarthy, M. M. (1993). "Challenges to the Public School Curriculum: New Targets and Strategies." Phi Delta Kappan, 75(1), 55-60.

McDermott, R. P. (1987). "Achieving School Failure: An Anthropological Approach to Illiteracy and Social Stratification." In G. D. Spindler (Ed.), Educational and Cultural Process: Anthropological Approaches (2nd ed., pp. 173-209). Prospect Heights, IL: Waveland.

Moll, L. C., Amanti, C., Neff, D., & González, N. (1992). "Funds of Knowledge for Teaching: Using a Qualitative Approach to Connect Homes and Classrooms." Theory Into Practice, 31, 132-141.

National Conference of Catholic Bishops. (1972). To Teach As Jesus Did. Washington DC: United States Catholic Conference.

Nieto, S. (1996). Affirming Diversity: The

Sociopolitical Context of Multicultural Education (2nd). New York: Longman.

Ogbu, J. U. (1987). "Variability in Minority Responses to Schooling: Nonimmigrants Vs. Immigrants." In G. Spindler & L. Spindler (Eds.), Interpretive Ethnography of Education: At Home and Abroad (pp. 255-280). New Jersey: Lawrence Erlbaum Associates.

Ogbu, J. U. (1992a). "Adaption to Minority Status and Impact on School Success." Theory Into Practice, 31, 287-295.

Ogbu, J. U. (1992b). "Understanding Cultural Diversity and Learning." Educational Researcher, 21(8), 5-14, 24.

Ogbu, J. U. (1993). "Difference in Cultural Frame of Reference." International Journal of Behavioral Development, 16, 483-506.

Ogbu, J. U., & Matute-Bianchi, M. E. (1986). "Understanding Sociocultural Factors: Knowledge, Identity and School Adjustment." In Beyond Language: Social and Cultural Factors in Schooling Language Minority Students (pp. 73-142). Los Angeles: Evaluation, Dissemination and Assessment Center, California State University, Los Angeles.

Pai, Y. (1990). Cultural Foundations of Education. New York: Merrill.

Payne, C. (1983). "Multicultural Education: A Natural Way to Teach." Contemporary Education, 54(2), 98-104.

Ramírez, M., III., & Castañeda, A. (1974). Cultural Democracy, Bicognitive Development and Education. New York: Academic Press.

Ravitch, D. (1990). "Multiculturalism: E Pluribus Plures." The American Scholar, 59, 337-334.

Rodriguez, R. (1982). Hunger of Memory: The Education of Richard Rodriguez. New York: Bantam Books.

Rueda, R. (1987). "Social and Communicative Aspects of Language Proficiency in Low-achieving Language Minority Students." In H. T. Trueba (Ed.), Success or Failure? Learning and the Language Minority Student (pp. 185-197). Cambridge, MA: Newbury House.

Rueda, R. (1990). "Assisted Performance in Writing Instruction with Learning-disabled Students." In L. C. Moll (Ed.), Vygotsky and Education: Instructional Implications and Applications of Sociohistorical Psychology (pp. 403-426). Cambridge, England: Cambridge University Press.

Rueda, R., & Moll, L. C. (1994). "A Sociocultural Perspective on Motivation." In H. F. O'Neil & M. Drillings (Eds.), Motivation: Theory and Research (pp. 117-137). Hillsdale, NJ: Lawrence Erlbaum Associates.

Savage, Frank X. (1995) United States Catholic Elementary & Secondary Schools 1995-96: Annual Statistical Report on School, Enrollment and Staffing. Washington DC: National Catholic Educational Association.

Scarcella, R. (1990). Teaching Language Minority Students in the Multicultural Classroom. New Jersey: Prentice Hall Regents.

Schlesinger, A. M., Jr. (1992). The Disuniting of America. New York: W. W. Norton.

Sleeter, C. E. (1989). "Multicultural Education as a Form of Resistance to Oppression." Journal of Education (Boston), 171(3), 51-71.

Sleeter, C. E. (Ed.). (1991). Empowerment Through Multicultural Education. Albany, NY: State University of New York Press.

Sleeter, C. E. (1993, March). "Multicultural Education: Five Views." The Education Digest, pp. 53-57.

Sleeter, C. E., & Grant, C. A. (1987). "An Analysis of Multicultural Education in the United States." Harvard Educational Review, 57, 421-444.

Sleeter, C. E., & Grant, C. A. (1988). Five Approaches to Race, Class and Gender. Columbus, OH: Merrill.

Sleeter, C. E., & McLaren, P. L. (Eds.). (1995). Multicultural Education, Critical Pedagogy, and the Politics of Difference. Albany, NY: State University of New York Press.

Steele, S. (1990). The Content of Our Character: A New Vision of Race in America. New York: Harper Collins.

Steele, S. (1992, July). "The New Sovereignty: Grievance Groups Have Become Nations Unto Themselves." Harper's Magazine, pp. 47-54.

Stigler, J. W., & Stevenson, H. W. (1991). "How Asian Teachers Polish Each Lesson to Perfection." American Educator, 15(1), 12-20, 43.

Suzuki, B. H. (1984). "Curriculum Transformation for Multicultural Education." Education And Urban Society, 16, 294-322.

Tharp, R., G., & Gallimore, R. (1988). Rousing Minds to Life: Teaching, Learning, and Schooling in Social Context. Cambridge: Cambridge University Press.

Trueba, H. T. (Ed.). (1987). Success or Failure? Learning and the Language Minority Student. Cambridge, MA: Newbury House.

Vélez-Ibáñez, C. G. (1988). "Networks of Exchange Among Mexicans in the U.S. and Mexico: Local Level Mediating Responses to National and International Transformations." Urban Anthropology, 17(1), 27-51.

Vélez-Ibáñez, C. G., & Greenberg, J. B. (1992). "Formation and Transformation of Funds of Knowledge Among U.S.-Mexican Households."

Anthropology & Education Quarterly, 24, 313-335.

Vogt, L. A., Jordan, C., & Tharp, R. G. (1987). "Explaining School Failure, Producing School Success: Two Cases.: Anthropology and Education Quarterly, 18, 276-286.

Vygotsky, L. S. (1978). Mind in Society: The Development of Higher Psychological Processes (M. Cole, V. John-Steiner, S. Scribner, & E. Souberman, Eds.). Cambridge, MA: Harvard University Press.

Wertsch, J. V. (Ed.). (1985a). Culture Communication, and Cognition: Vygotskian Perspectives. Cambridge, London: Cambridge University Press.

Wertsch, J. V. (1985b). Vygotsky and the Social Formation of Mind. Cambridge, MA: Harvard University Press.

Wiles, J. W. (1993). Promoting Change in Schools: Ground Level Practices that Work. New York: Scholastic.

Witkin, H. A. (1967). "A Cognitive Style Approach to Cross-cultural Research." Journal of Psychology, 2, 233-250.

APPENDIX A

Suggestions for Professional Development and Faculty In-Service Workshops Regarding Cultural Diversity

Bringing in well-known speakers and professional development personnel for faculty in-services regarding cultural diversity is not always possible for schools. Expense or the availability of resource persons can be a prohibiting factor. Obviously, receiving support and ideas from more competent others from outside the school is helpful. However, schools can do many things to encourage professional development using existing resources and community assistance. The following suggestions are designed for "in house" faculty in-services sessions.

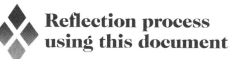

Reflection process using this document

Cultural Diversity in Catholic Schools: Challenges and Opportunities for Catholic Educators (Martin, this volume), could be used as the basis for a faculty in-service. The following is a suggested outline of a reflection process using the publication.

Focus questions prior to reading the document

It is helpful to invite faculty, staff and administrators to reflect on several focus questions prior to reading the document. These questions help set the context for the reading and focus the subsequent discussion. These questions and document can be given to the faculty several weeks before the faculty in-service.

- What is my personal philosophy regarding teaching and learning?
- How does the context of Catholic education influence my work?
- Which former teachers were especially helpful and empowering? What methods, teaching strategies and approaches did they use that were effective?
- Which former teachers were not helpful or empowering? Why was this the case?
- What are my hopes and desires for each student in my classroom? In the school?

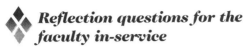

Reflection questions for the faculty in-service

After each faculty member, staff member or administrator has read and reflected on the document, an in-service session (or several sessions) can provide for further reflection, discussion and networking with other faculty. I would suggest a format that allows for both small group sharing and large group processing. In schools with larger faculties and staffs, it may be helpful to invite one to three faculty or staff members to prepare the questions and share their responses with the entire group at the onset of the day in order to model a deeper level of sharing and to "prime the pump" for further reflection. It may be helpful to ask the faculty members to keep a journal during the in-service process in which they would record their answers to the pre-service and in-service questions.

- Why did I get into teaching in a Catholic school? What keeps me coming back?
- What are the realities of cultural diversity in my classroom? In my school? In my community? How do I feel about the changes in demographics?
- What did I find helpful in the publication? What did I learn?
- What was not helpful in the publication and why?
- How important is it for me as a Catholic educator to be culturally sensitive to those from cultural backgrounds different from my own? What strategies or methods could I employ that would enable me to become more culturally sensitive?

- How can having a sociocultural perspective influence my teaching? My work in education?
- What are the *funds of knowledge* that the students at my school bring to the setting? How can I be more aware of their funds of knowledge? How can I utilize students' funds of knowledge to better educate them?
- The constructivist approach emphasizes active participation by students in the process of constructing knowledge. How could this idea influence my teaching and interaction with students?
- What is the *hidden curriculum* in my classroom? In the school? How welcoming is the classroom and school culture to all students?
- How can Gospel values influence my response to cultural diversity? Does the particular context of Catholic education make any difference in my beliefs and attitudes toward cultural diversity?

❖ Ongoing reflection activities

In responding to issues regarding cultural diversity, engaging in personal reflection is important. Reflecting on how prejudice, bias or discrimination may be influencing one's behavior, despite good intentions, is helpful for each educator. All of us have areas of bias and prejudice; to the extent that we act upon these we might be practicing discrimination. The following reflection questions are designed to help identify these issues. These questions might be used for personal reflection, before a faculty in-service on cultural diversity, or as an ongoing process of reflection during the course of a school year. Discussing these questions with a "learning partner" would also be appropriate for educators.

Teachers could consider the following questions:

- What kinds of materials do I use in my teaching? Are they reflective of the diversity in the school, in the community, in the country?
- What is my philosophy concerning learning and teaching?
- Do I believe that every student can learn?
- Do I believe that every student comes to school with a culture and prior experiences that are valuable and can contribute to the learning process?
- How often do I allow students to be responsible for, excited about, and actually direct their own learning?
- How often do I discuss learning and teaching issues with students? Do I take the time to ask them for their opinion about what works in the educational process?
- What is my class room environment like? Is it welcoming and affirming of the students in the school—including those from minority backgrounds? Do students have a voice in my classroom?
- How much of my teaching is connected to meaningful content that relates to the everyday interests and experiences of my students and how much is simply abstract and decontextualized instruction?

For administrators I would suggest the following reflection questions:

- What is the school culture in the school? Do all students feel welcomed and valued in the school? Does everyone feel that he or she has a place to connect?
- Do our school activities and extracurricular activities foster cultural diversity and also build community? Is there tension among different ethnic groups? How do I (we) deal with this?
- Do hiring practices reflect the diversity of the school and the community? Do students have adequate role models?
- Do admission policies reflect the diversity of the community? Do ethnic minority students feel they are welcome to apply at the school? Are there special issues for the recruitment and retention of ethnic minority students (language issues, immigration issues, etc.)? Do admissions brochures and other related materials reflect acceptance of cultural differences?
- Is adequate counseling provided for all students? Does the school provide counselors who are culturally sensitive and competent for ethnic minority students?
- What is the school's relationship with the local community? Do all families and parents feel comfortable and welcome at school events? Are there language or cultural differences that keep parents from responding to the school?
- Are opportunities provided for teacher training in cultural diversity? How committed is

the school to providing ongoing professional development in the areas of culturally sensitive instruction, multicultural education, cooperative learning?
- Is there a forum to discuss issues of cultural diversity on the campus and to evaluate the school's progress in this area? Perhaps, a committee of faculty, staff, students, and administrators would be helpful.

For all educators to consider personally:
- What is my attitude toward people of different ethnic and cultural backgrounds? Do I have any unexamined prejudices that may influence my professional behavior? Am I sending any unintentional signals to students and parents about my attitudes?
- How culturally sensitive am I to the diverse cultures in the school? Are there occasions or events that I could attend that would provide greater cross-cultural experiences?

Review relevant literature

The educational literature regarding cultural diversity has developed greatly since the 1980s and includes many helpful and insightful works. Many of the works cited in this document could be helpful for educators to review in greater detail. Appendix B includes a bibliography of additional works that might be of interest to the Catholic school teacher. One suggestion is to identify and locate relevant literature and have the faculty, staff, and administration read and discuss it. A practical way to facilitate this for the busy professional is to use "learning partners": two people could read the same article, discuss it, and talk about ways of implementation for a particular school setting. After the faculty has completed this process, individual members could present what they learned to the entire faculty and share ideas about implementation. This process could take the course of an academic year, and could be repeated several times.

However, there is one caveat regarding the above process. While there are many articles relating to cultural diversity, choosing carefully from the literature is important. Not all of the literature concerning cultural diversity is of equal merit, and in some cases articles might not be appropriate or helpful in the context of Catholic schools or in a particular setting. In order for the above suggestion to work, therefore, the selection of the material is crucial. It would be unfortunate if a faculty member was turned off to cultural diversity issues because of in-service content that was inappropriate or not well constructed. Perhaps a committee of interested faculty could help to identify and locate appropriate articles and make them available to the faculty. The literature can include both general articles about responding to cultural diversity and articles that are specific to a particular discipline or an issue in the school.

◆ Utilize community resources

Often resources for faculty in-service programs regarding cultural diversity exist in local communities and are not fully utilized. Certainly, local university and college faculties might be available to assist in professional development but, at times, cost can make this impractical. Some university faculty members have provided such services to inner-city schools on a *pro bono* basis, and it is often worth inquiring. Furthermore, business and political leaders in the community might be available to assist in professional development.

In addition to the above resource persons, parents and other community members can offer valuable insights into issues of cultural diversity. Including community members in professional development concerning cultural diversity helps to utilize the community's funds of knowledge. Parents and other community members have important experiences and perspectives that relate to cultural diversity. The perspective of ethnic minority parents, recent immigrants and community members can be especially helpful for the faculty to hear. Inviting these people to "tell their story" to the faculty can be very powerful. Such presentations can be followed by discussion and dialogue. Inviting community members to assist in professional development also helps the school build a bridge to ethnic minority communities, which helps to influence the school culture positively.

APPENDIX B

**Additional Resources for Educators
Interested in Cultural Diversity**

Banks, J. A., & Banks, C. A., McGee (Eds.). (1993). <u>Multicultural Education: Issues and Perspectives</u> (2nd ed.). Boston: Allyn and Bacon.

Banks, C. A., & Banks, J. A. (1995). Equity pedagogy: An Essential Component of Multicultural Education. <u>Theory Into Practice,</u> *34,* 152-158.

Bartoli, J. S. (1995). <u>Unequal Opportunity.</u> New York: Teachers College Press.

Beauboeuf-Lafontant, T., & Augustine, D. S. (Eds.). (1996). Facing Racism in Education. <u>Harvard Educational Review</u> Reprint Series No.

28. Cambridge, MA: Harvard Educational Review.

Bennett, C. I. (1995). Comprehensive Multicultural Education: Theory and Practice (3rd ed.). Boston: Allyn and Bacon.

Campbell, D. E. (1996). Choosing Democracy. Englewood Cliffs, NJ: Merrill Publishing.

Cushner, K., McClelland, A., & Safford, P. (1996). Human Diversity in Education: An Integrative Approach (2nd ed.). New York: McGraw-Hill.

Díaz-Rico, L. T., & Weed, K. Z. (1995). The Crosscultural, Language, and Academic Development Handbook. Boston: Allyn and Bacon.

DeVillar, R. A., Faltis, C. J., & Cummins, J. P. (Eds.). (1994). Cultural Diversity in Schools: From Rhetoric to Practice. Albany, NY: State University of New York Press.

García, E. E., & McLaughlin, B. (Eds.). (1995). Yearbook in Early Childhood Education. Vol. 6: Meeting the Challenge of Linguistic and Cultural Diversity in Early Childhood Education. New York: Teachers College Press.

Gay, G. (1994). At the Essence of Learning: Multicultural Education. West Lafayette, IN: Kappa Delta Phi.

Geismar, K., & Nicoleau, G. (Eds.). (1993). Teaching for Change: Addressing Issues of Difference in the College Classroom. Cambridge, MA: Harvard Educational Review.

Grant, C., & Sleeter, C. A. (1989). Turning on Learning: Five Approaches for Multicultural Teaching Plans for Race, Class, Gender, and Disability. Columbus, OH: Merrill Publishing.

Grant, C. A. (Ed.). (1992). Research & Multicultural Education: From the Margins to the Mainstream. London: Falmer Press.

Grant, C. A., & Gomez, M. L. (1996). Making Schooling Multicultural: Campus and Classroom. Englewood Cliffs, NJ: Prentice Hall.

Heath, S. B., & McLaughlin, M. W. (Eds.). (1993). Identity and Inner-city Youth: Beyond Ethnicity and Gender. New York: Teachers College Press.

Hollins, E. R., King, J. E., & Hayman, W. C. (Eds.). (1994). Teaching Diverse Populations: Formulating a Knowledge Base. Albany, NY: New York State University Press.

Jackson, O. R. (1985). Dignity and Solidarity: An Introduction to Peace and Justice Education. Chicago: Loyola University Press.

Kendall, F. E. (1996). Diversity in the Classroom: New Approaches to the Education of Young Children (2nd ed.). New York: Teachers College Press.

LaBelle, T. J., & Ward, C. R. (1994). Multiculturalism and Education: Diversity and Its Impact on Schools and Society. Albany, NY: State University of New York Press.

Ladson-Billings, G. (1995). Culturally Relevant Teaching [Special Issue]. Theory Into Practice, 34.

Ladson-Billings, G. (1995). But That's Just Good Teaching! The Case for Culturally Relevant Pedagogy. Theory Into Practice, 34, 159-166.

Larkin, J. M., & Sleeter, C. E. (Eds.). (1995). Developing Multicultural Teacher Education Curricula. Albany, NY: State University of New York Press.

Levinson, B. A., Foley, D. E., & Holland, D. C. (Eds.). (1996). The Cultural Production of the Educated Person: Critical Ethnographies and Schooling and Local Practice. Albany, NY: State University of New York Press.

Lincoln, Y. S. (1995). Learning from students' voices. Theory Into Practice, 34, 88-93.

Manning, M. L., & Baruth, L. G. (1996). Multicultural Education (2nd ed.). Boston: Allyn and Bacon.

McLeod, B. (Ed.). (1994). Language and Learning. Albany, NY: State University of New York Press.

Minami, M., & Kennedy, B. P. (Eds.). (1991). Language Issues in Literacy and Bilingual/ Multicultural Education. Harvard Educational Review Reprint Series No. 22. Cambridge, MA: Harvard Educational Review.

Nava, A., Molina, H., Cabello, B., De La Torre, B., & Vega-Castañeda, L. (1994). Educating Americans in a Multicultural Society (2nd ed.). New York: McGraw-Hill.

Nieto, S. (1996). Affirming Diversity: The Sociopolitical Context of Multicultural Education (2nd ed.). White Plains, NY: Longman Publishers.

Noya, G. C., Geismar, K., & Nicoleau, G. (Eds.). (1995). Shifting Histories: Transforming Education for Social Change. Cambridge, MA: Harvard Educational Review.

Oldfather, P. (1995). Learning from Students' Voices [Special Issue]. Theory Into Practice, 34.

Phelan, P., & Davidson, A. L. (Eds.). (1993). Renegotiating Cultural Diversity in American Schools. New York: Teachers College Press.

Pignatelli, F., & Pflaum, S. W. (1994). Experiencing Diversity: Toward Educational Equity. Thousand Oaks, CA: Corwin Press.

Richard-Amato, P. A., & Snow, M. A. (1992). The Multicultural Classroom: Readings for Content-area Teachers. White Plains, NY: Longman

Publishing.

Seelye, N. H. (1993). Teaching Culture: Strategies for Intercultural Communication (3rd ed.). Lincolnwood, IL: National Textbook Company.

Sleeter, C. E. (Ed.). (1991). Empowerment Through Multicultural Education. Albany, NY: State University of New York Press.

Sleeter, C., & Grant, C. A. (1993). Making Choices for Multicultural Education: Five Approaches to Race, Class, and Gender (2nd ed.). Columbus, OH: Merrill Publishing.

Sleeter, C. E., & McLaren, P. L. (Eds.). (1995). Multicultural Education, Critical Pedagogy, and the Politics of Difference. Albany, NY: State University of New York Press.

Tiedt, P. L., & Tiedt, I. M. (1995). Multicultural Teaching: A Handbook of Activities, Information, and Resources (4th ed.). Boston: Allyn and Bacon.

Trueba, H. T., Rodriguez, C., Zou, Y., & Cintrón, J. (1993). Healing Multicultural America: Mexican Immigrants Rise to Power in Rural California. Washington, DC: Falmer Press.

Trueba, H. T., Cheng, L. R., Lilly, & Ima, K. (1993). Myth or Reality: Adaptive Strategies of Asian Americans in California. Washington, DC: Falmer Press.

Wang, M. C., & Reynolds, M. C. (Eds.). (1995). <u>Making a Difference for Students at Risk: Trends and Alternatives.</u> Thousand Oaks, CA: Corwin Press.

APPENDIX C
Internet Addresses Concerning Cultural Diversity

The following Internet addresses might be useful to educators who wish to learn more about diversity and available resources. These addresses are provided for informational purposes only, and neither the author nor NCEA makes any particular endorsement of home pages or programs. Some of the descriptions are quoted directly from the homepage, and are so indicated by quotation marks.

1. African Americans Resources
http://scuish.scu.edu/SCU/Programs/Diversity/african.html
Listings of resources.

2. American Educational Research Association (AERA)

http://tikkun.ed.asu.edu/aera/home.html

This homepage presents the various divisions and Special Interests Groups (SIG's) of the American Educational Research Association, the premier research association in the field of education. Of special interest is Division G, the Social Context of Education.

3. American Studies Web: Race and Ethnicity

http://pantheon.cis.yale.edu/~davidp/race.html

Contains numerous links to ethnic studies and related issues.

4. Asian American Resources

http://scuish.scu.edu/SCU/Programs/Diversity/asian.html

Listings of resources.

5. Ask ERIC Virtual Library

http://ericir.sunsite.syr.edu/

This homepage provides an easy entry way into the ERIC system. It allows a user to search the ERIC database, answers questions regarding ERIC, and features a section on research and development.

6. The Association for Supervision and Curriculum Development (ASCD) Web

http://www.ascd.org/

"ASCD is an international, nonprofit, nonpartisan education association committed to the

mission of forging covenants in teaching and learning for the success of all learners. Founded in 1943, ASCD provides professional development in curriculum and supervision; initiates and supports activities to provide educational equity for all students; and serves as a world-class leader in education information services."

"ASCD's 198,000 members, who reside in more than 100 countries, include superintendents, supervisors, principals, teachers, professors of education, school board members, students, and parents who share a commitment to quality education and a belief that all students can learn in a well-planned educational program. These dedicated individuals make ASCD one of the largest professional education associations in the world."

7. AWARE Resources (A World Aware, Reality Education)
   http://www.geocities.com/Athens/7100/aware.html

AWARE provides K-12 multicultural education and cultural diversity training for education and business.

8. Boston College Center for International Higher Education
   http://www.bc.edu/bc_org/avp/soe/cihe/Center.html

"The Boston College Center for International Higher Education provides information and support for international initiatives in higher education. Focusing especially on academic in-

stitutions in the Jesuit tradition, the Center is dedicated to comparative and international higher education worldwide."

9. The BUENO Center for Multicultural Education
http://www.colorado.edu/BUENO/bueno_index.html

"The BUENO Center for Multicultural Education strongly promotes quality education with an emphasis on the value of cultural pluralism in our schools through a comprehensive range of research, training and service projects. The Center is deeply committed to facilitating equal educational opportunities for cultural and language minority students. The Center also disseminates research findings and related information through various Center publications. The Center is an integral part of the School of Education at the University of Colorado at Boulder. Funding for some Center programs is provided through grants and contracts from the U.S. Department of Education."

10. California Ethnic and Multicultural Archives
http://www.library.ucsb.edu/speccoll/cema.html

A homepage sponsored by U.C. Santa Barbara that provides links to numerous homepages that deal with diversity in the California context.

11. The Center for Excellence in Education
http://cee.indiana.edu/

"The Center for Excellence in Education at Indiana University, is an organization dedicated to helping people find the appropriate application of technology to improve teaching and learning in diverse settings."

12. Educational Interface
http://www.cis.uab.edu/info/grads/mmf/EdPage/EdPage2.html

"The goal of this interface is to provide the K-12 Educational Community with a resource for organized and efficient access to the World Wide Web."

13. Engines for Education
http://www.ils.nwu.edu/~e_for_e/nodes/EDU-CATOR-pg.html

The network site discusses educational reform and gives suggestions and recommendations. Of particular interests are the sections discussing learning as meaningful activity and cultural literacy.

14. ERIC Clearinghouse on Assessment and Evaluation
http://www.cua.edu/www/eric_ae/

The ERIC Clearinghouse on Assessment and Evaluation seeks to provide 1) balanced information concerning educational assessment and 2) resources to encourage responsible test use.

15. ERIC Clearinghouse on Urban Education
http://eric-web.tc.columbia.edu/home_files/
pub_list.html

Clearinghouse for sources relevent to urban and minority education.

16. ERIC Digest, "Varieties of Multicultural education: An Introduction," by Gary Burnett, ERIC Clearinghouse on Urban Education, New York, N.Y.
http://eric-web.tc.columbia.edu/digests/
dig98.html

This ERIC Digest discusses the many uses of the term "multicultural education,' and refers to the models approach used by scholars to better understand multicultural education.

17. European American Resources
http://scuish.scu.edu/SCU/Programs/Diversity/
euros.html

Listings of resources.

18. Gonzaga University, Multicultural resources
http://www.rosauer.gonzaga.edu/~multicult/
multi.html

A homepage provided by Gonzaga University with links to other homepages dealing with ethnic and cultural diversity.

19. Kids on Campus
http://www.tc.cornell.edu/Kids.on.Campus/

"For the past six years, the Cornell Theory Center has sponsored Kids On Campus as part

of our celebration of National Science and Technology Week. The purpose of this event is to increase computer awareness and scientific interest among Ithaca area third, fourth, and fifth grade students. We want to introduce computing to children in ways they can enjoy and understand. Hands-on computer activities, innovative videos, and exciting demonstrations help the children develop interest and excitement in computers and science. The exhibits are presented by Cornell University faculty and staff, and area science organizations."

20. Latino/a Resources
http://scuish.scu.edu/SCU/Programs/Diversity/latinos.html

Listings of resources.

21. Learning Research and Development Center (LRDC)
http://www.lrdc.pitt.edu/

Since its founding in 1963, LRDC has probed the nature of thinking, knowing, and understanding in and beyond school. Its twofold mission has been to broaden our scientific insights into all aspects of learning and to support the use of research in instructional settings as varied as classrooms, industry, and museums.

22. Middle Eastern American Resources
http://scuish.scu.edu/SCU/Programs/Diversity/mideast.html

Listings of resources.

23. The Mind, Culture, and Activity Homepage
http://communication.ucsd.edu/MCA/
index.html

"The Mind, Culture, and Activity Homepage is an interactive forum for a community of interdisciplinary scholars who share an interest in the study of the human mind in its cultural and historical contexts. Our emphasis is research that seeks to resolve methodological problems associated with the analysis of human and theoretical approaches that place culture and activity at the center of attempts to understand human nature. Our participants come from a variety of disciplines, including, anthropology, cognitive science, education, linguistics, psychology and sociology."

24. Multicultural Alliance Homepage
http://branson.org/mca.old/mca.mission.html

"In 1989, fifteen Bay Area independent schools created the Multicultural.Alliance. Its mission: To help public and private schools increase and support racial, cultural and ethnic diversity within.their institutions. Educational institutions committed to addressing the issues of race and culture join the Alliance by paying yearly membership dues and participating in alliance sponsored projects."

25. Multicultural Book Review Page
http://www.isomedia.com/homes/jmele/
homepage.html

"The purpose of this page is to create a qualitative list of multicultural literature for K-12

educators. We would like to avoid presenting just lists of books, but instead give educators a chance to find out a little more information about multicultural literature others have used successfully."

26. The Multicultural Center
http://144.96.228.38/

27. Multicultural Pavillion Teacher's Corner
http://curry.edschool.virginia.edu/go/multicultural/teachers.html

The University of Viginia's Multicultural Pavilion Teacher's Corner provides resources specific to K-12 teachers of all subjects, focusing on diversity issues.

28. National Center for Research on Cultural Diversity and Second Language Learning
http://zzyx.ucsc.edu/Cntr/cntr.html

"The National Center for Research on Cultural Diversity and Second Language Learning is a U.S. Department of Education research center located on the campus of the University of California, Santa Cruz. The National Center for Research on Cultural Diversity and Second Language Learning is funded by the Office of Educational Research and Improvement of the U.S. Department of Education to conduct research on the education of language minority students in the United States. The Center is operated by the University of California, Santa Cruz, through the University of California's statewide Linguistic Minority Research Institute (LMRI), in collaboration with a number of

other institutions nationwide.

The Center is committed to promoting the intellectual development, literacy, and thoughtful citizenship of language minority students and to increasing appreciation of the cultural and linguistic diversity of the American people. Center researchers from a variety of disciplines are conducting studies across the country with participants from a wide range of language minority groups in pre-kindergarten through grade 12 classrooms. Research projects deal with the relationship between first and second language learning; the relationship between cultural and linguistic factors in the achievement of literacy; teaching strategies to help children from diverse linguistic and cultural backgrounds gain access to content material; alternate models of assessment for language minority students; various instructional models for language minority children; and the effect of modifications in the social organization of schools on the academic performance of students from diverse backgrounds."

29. The National Foreign Language Resource Center
  http://128.171.23.249/nflrc/

"Under a grant from the U.S. Department of Education, the National Foreign Language Resource Center at the University of Hawaii has since 1990 served as one of a small number of resource centers established to improve and enrich foreign language education nationwide. The Center engages in research and materials

development projects and conducts summer institutes for language professionals. In addition, the Center's publications division distributes teaching materials, as well as a series of technical and research reports. Drawing on the abundance of Asian-Pacific resources afforded by its locale, the Center focuses its efforts on the less commonly taught languages, particularly those of Asia and the Pacific, recognizing that competence in these languages is increasingly vital to the Nation's future."

30. Native American Cultural Resources on the Internet
http://hanksville.phast.umass.edu/misc/NAculture.html

Listing of resources.

31. Native American Resources
http://scuish.scu.edu/SCU/Programs/Diversity/native.html

Listings of resources.

32. Resources for Educators
http://olam.ed.asu.edu/~casey/links.html

This webpage provides numerous links to important sites for educators.

33. Santa Clara University Diversity Homepage
http://scuish.scu.edu/SCU/Programs/Diversity/homepage.html

A homepage sponsored by the Santa Clara University with links to other homepages that deal with diversity issues.

34. United States Department of Education
http://www.ed.gov/

This webpage gives information on educational programs, grants and other opportunities.

35. Vygotsky: A Learning Construction Zone
http://www.ced.appstate.edu/

"The purpose of Vygotsky is to provide information about projects that are applying technology to research and development on learning environments and to share the results of this work. All projects are housed in the Learning and Technology Laboratory (LTL) of the College of Education of Appalachian State University. These projects are made possible through the Appalachian State University/Public School Partnership, the Appalachian Rural Systemic Initiative, funded by the National Science Foundation, the Mellon Foundation, and the BellSouth Foundation."

36. The Web of Culture
http://www.worldculture.com/

A homepage dedicated to cross-cultural communication and information. Contains information on world languages, currencies, religions, holidays, customs, and other aspects of culture.

ABOUT THE AUTHOR

❖

A former elementary and high school teacher, Shane Martin, SJ, PhD, currently serves as an assistant professor of education at Loyola Marymount University, Los Angeles, California. His published pieces and other professional experiences reflect his interest in the relationship between cultural diversity and Catholic secondary education. Father Martin is a frequent presenter at conferences sponsored by the American Educational Research Association, the National Catholic Educational Association and the American Association of Colleges for Teacher Education.